V-MAIL

LETTERS FROM THE ROMANS AT VINDOLANDA FORT NEAR HADRIAN'S WALL

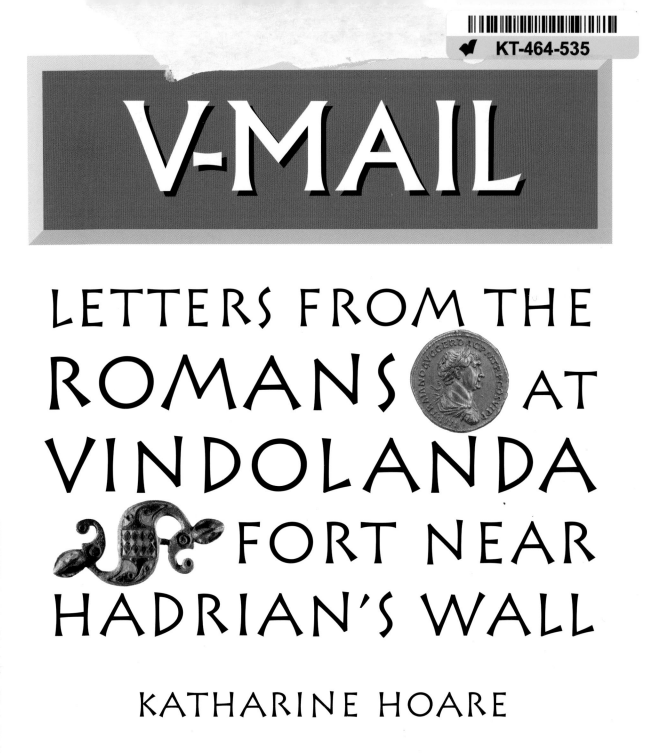

KATHARINE HOARE

THE BRITISH MUSEUM PRESS

© 2008 The Trustees of the British Museum

First published in Great Britain in 2008 by British Museum Press
A division of The British Museum Company Ltd
38 Russell Square, London WC1B 3QQ

ISBN 978 0 7141 3134 4

Katharine Hoare has asserted the right to be identified as the author of this work.
A catalogue record for this title is available from the British Library.

Designed and typeset by Eric Drewery
Printed and bound in Italy by Printer Trento

Mixed Sources
Product group from well-managed
forests and other controlled sources
www.fsc.org Cert no. CQ-COC-000012
© 1996 Forest Stewardship Council

FSC

Illustration acknowledgements
All photographs are © the Trustees of the British Museum, taken by members of the
British Museum Photography and Imaging Dept, unless otherwise stated below.

p. 4 map: ML Design.
p. 6 top: Paul Gardner.
p. 9 top left: John Green.
p. 10 bottom: William Webb.
p. 14 bottom: Victor Ambrus.
p. 17 bottom: William Webb.
p. 19 bottom right: John Green.
p. 21: bottom: Karen Hughes.
p. 22 top left: Karen Hughes.
p. 26 top right: Katharine Hoare.
p. 29 top left: William Webb.
p. 31 centre and bottom: Andrew Malone.

CONTENTS

THE ROMANS

Rome started between 2000 and 1000 BC as a group of farming villages near the River Tiber in Italy. The villages grew wealthy from trade and during the 700s BC joined together to become one town which grew into the city of Rome.

THE ROMAN EMPIRE

Vindolanda

Rome

ROMAN EMPIRE

Rome began to conquer land around the city, and by 270 BC it controlled all the Italian peninsula. Over the next 250 years, the Romans built up a vast empire. The map shows the Roman empire at its largest (during the reign of the emperor Trajan from AD 98 to 117). It included land in Europe, Africa and Asia.

The empire brought Rome great power and wealth. Around the time that the first Vindolanda fort was built, the Romans were constructing buildings such as the Colosseum, a huge amphitheatre for public entertainment, in Rome itself.

ROMAN BRITAIN

Julius Caesar led two military expeditions to Britain in 55 and 54 BC during which the Romans made links with some British rulers who began to enjoy Roman wine, use Roman pottery like this and even visit Rome.

Then in AD 46, under the emperor Claudius, a Roman invasion force landed in southern England to make Britain part of the empire. This coin, made to celebrate the Roman victory, shows a triumphal arch with Claudius on horseback on top. The letters DE BRITANN say 'A triumph over Britain' in Latin. Britain remained a Roman province until about AD 410.

VINDOLANDA

The Romans built a fort at Vindolanda around AD 85 to help control the northern frontier of the province. About 40 years later Hadrian's Wall was built as a military border between Roman Britain and the land further north in Scotland. Although Vindolanda was several miles south of the Wall, it became a Wall fort between Housesteads and Great Chesters.

Early forts at Vindolanda were built from wood and had to be rebuilt every eight years or so. By the time Hadrian's Wall was built, there had been five forts at Vindolanda. In total, at least eight forts were built, one on top of the other! The fort was used until the end of Roman rule around AD 410. Over the next 200 years Vindolanda was still occupied, as local authorities tried to control the people to the north.

THE VINDOLANDA TABLETS

The early wooden forts at Vindolanda now lie about four metres below the ground under the remains of later stone forts. Before building each new fort the Romans put clay and turf over the demolished remains of the old fort. This has helped objects to survive in the ground. Archaeologists are still digging up new things.

The Vindolanda tablets are thin pieces of wood, covered with ink handwriting. They include personal letters and official military documents. The first group of tablets was found in a waterlogged rubbish heap in 1973. Since then 100s more have been recovered.

The tablets were usually less than 3 mm thick and about 20 cm wide by 9 cm high (the size of a large postcard). The text was written with a reed pen, using ink stored in ink-wells like this one. This has the owner's name, Iucundus, scratched on it. The tablets were folded to protect the writing and the address was written on the outside. Longer documents were made by punching holes in the corners and tying several tablets together. The letters were written in Latin.

Most of the tablets date from about AD 92–105 when the fort was occupied by the 1st Cohort of Tungrians and the 9th Cohort of Batavians. Soldiers from the 3rd Cohort of Batavians and Spanish cavalry might also have spent some time at Vindolanda.

6

HADRIAN'S WALL

Hadrian's Wall was a defensive barrier that guarded the northern frontier of the province. It stretched for 73 miles between Segedunum (Wallsend) in the east and Bowness-on-Solway in the west.

This building stone has the inscription LEG II AVG, a military standard, Pegasus (the winged horse) and a goat emblem. It records the work done by soldiers from the Second Legion Augusta (based at Caerleon, Wales) sent to help build Hadrian's Wall.

This small pan is decorated with a design thought to show Hadrian's Wall. Around the top are the names of five forts at the west end of the Wall: MAIS (Bowness-on-Solway), ABALLAVA (Burgh-by-Sands), VXELODUM (Stanwix), CAMBOGLANS (Castlesteads), BANNA (Birdoswald).

HADRIAN (reigned AD 117–138)

Emperor Hadrian travelled extensively around the empire. While visiting Britain in AD 122 he ordered the building of Hadrian's Wall.

18 May, total number of the 1st Cohort of Tungrians, whose commander is Iulius Verecundus, is 752 (including 6 centurions). Those absent are: 46 guards of the governor in London; 337 at the office of Ferox at Corbridge (including 2 centurions); 1 centurion in London. Total absentees are 456 (including 5 centurions). The remainder present is 296 (including 1 centurion) of whom 31 are unfit for duty being sick, wounded or suffering from inflammation of the eyes. Fit for active service are 265 (including 1 centurion).

This tablet is a report on the 1st Cohort of Tungrians. It may be a monthly list to keep Iulius Verecundus, the commanding officer, informed about his soldiers. About half of the soldiers are away from the fort, including 337 soldiers at Corbridge fort (known to the Romans as Coria) and a centurion who is in London on a special mission. 296 soldiers remain at the fort, although 31 of these are ill.

As well as the auxiliary foot-soldiers, there may have been cavalry soldiers and their horses at Vindolanda. This bronze cavalry helmet has side plates to protect the cheeks and a neck guard at the back. A cavalry sword was longer than the sword usually carried by a soldier in the legions.

The Roman army included two different types of military units – legions and auxiliary regiments. A legion consisted of about 5,000 legionary soldiers (left) and centurions commanded by a senior officer, all of whom were Roman citizens.

The soldiers at Vindolanda fort were auxiliary soldiers (right). Auxiliary regiments contained 500 or 1,000 soldiers (commanded by a Roman officer) divided into cohorts (commanded by a prefect) and centuries (commanded by a centurion). Auxiliaries were not Roman citizens.

Forts were permanent bases for the army. They were protected by a wall and a ditch with roads running into the fort through gateways in the wall. At the centre was the military headquarters. Other buildings included houses for the commander and senior officers, workshops, store-rooms, stables, baths, toilets, rows of barracks where the soldiers slept and

sometimes a hospital. This is a reconstruction of the gateway of Arbeia Roman Fort at South Shields.

On this coin Hadrian is speaking to the army of Britain. He is on horseback and holds his hand above his head to attract the attention of the soldiers in front of him. The writing says EXERC[ITVS] BRITANNICVS (army of Britain).

9

WORK AND TRADES

24 April, in the workshops 343 men including: shoemakers 12; builders to the bath-house 18; lead working, saw-makers, builders to the hospital, workers to the kilns, plasterer.

This tablet records the number of soldiers doing different jobs at the fort. It shows that most of the soldiers worked in the workshops when not on active campaign. Other jobs listed are mainly to do with construction work. It may be that the soldiers were building a new and larger fort. Other soldiers would be working on routine tasks such as cleaning, cooking, washing clothes and feeding the horses.

A wide range of specialist skills were employed at Vindolanda so the garrison could look after a lot of its own needs. However, not everything could be made or repaired at the fort.

One tablet records the purchase of parts for a wagon. These were probably used for making or mending wagons at the fort. The tablets mention two vets called Virilis and Alio, a shield-maker called Lucius, a doctor called Marcus and a brewer called Atrectus all working at Vindolanda.

At the centre of a Roman shield was a bronze boss to protect the surface of the shield during battle. The shield itself was made from wood and leather and if necessary the boss could be transferred to a new shield. This boss, found near the River Tyne, belonged to a soldier from the 8th Legion called Junius Dubitatus who marked his name on the edge. The fort workshops would have been able to repair other pieces of armour too.

This carpentry tool would have been used for cutting and shaping wood. It also has a hammer at one end for banging in nails.

> The Britons are unprotected by armour. There are very many cavalry. The cavalry do not use swords nor do the wretched Britons mount in order to throw javelins.

This tablet describes how the native Britons fight. It might be an intelligence report or information collected before recruiting Britons into the Roman army. The Roman army usually stationed soldiers away from their home region so a British unit would not have served at Vindolanda itself. The writer of this report uses the word *Brittunculi* which means 'little Britons'. It implies that the writer does not think much of the local people.

A civilian settlement, known as a *vicus*, often grew up next to a fort. People who lived in the *vicus* would trade and socialize with the soldiers. This tombstone was found in a *vicus* near the Roman fort at Old Penrith, Cumbria. It commemorates Marcus Cocceius Nonnus who died age 6.

To show that Britain was part of the Roman empire, the Romans put a figure called Britannia on some of their coins. This female figure represented the Roman province of Britain and is still used on some British coins today.

Roman auxiliary soldiers were normally recruited from new provinces or areas outside the Empire. They were not usually Roman citizens but were granted citizenship after 25 years of service. Some of the soldiers at Vindolanda were Batavians, a group of people who lived in what is nowadays the Netherlands. They were well known for their horse-riding skills and formed part of the invasion force which arrived in Britain in AD 46.

During the AD 200s a unit of cavalrymen from North Africa was based at Aballava fort (Burgh-by-Sands) on Hadrian's Wall. They were probably brought over by the emperor Septimius Severus (reigned AD 193–211) who was also from North Africa.

Archaeologists think that auxiliary troops would often take the clothing and customs of their home region with them as they travelled the empire. On the other hand, local people in a province might be influenced by the Roman way of life. For example, this painted portrait shows somebody who lived in Egypt when it was a Roman province. He has a Roman hairstyle similar to the one on this statue of the emperor Tiberius.

FRIENDS AND FAMILY

This tablet is a birthday invitation sent by Claudia Severa to Sulpicia Lepidina. Claudia Severa is obviously looking forward to her birthday on 11 September and seems to be planning a small party with her friend. She also passes on good wishes from her husband and son.

Claudia Severa to her Lepidina greetings. On 11 September, for the day of the celebration of my birthday, I give you a warm invitation to make sure that you come to us, it will make the day more enjoyable for me if you are present. Give my greetings to your Cerialis. My Aelius and my little son send him their greetings. I shall expect you.

In another tablet Claudia Severa writes to Sulpicia Lepidina to discuss another visit. This time Claudia is going to see Sulpicia. She explains that she has things to talk about which she does not want to write down in a letter. These letters show that Claudia and Sulpicia wrote to each other regularly and are the earliest known examples of handwriting in Latin by women.

Claudia Severa was the wife of Aelius Brocchus, a senior army officer. Army commanders, unlike their soldiers, took their families with them when they were sent to a fort away from their home. Their children might have played with wooden toys such as this horse, found in Egypt and dating from the time when Egypt was part of the Roman empire.

The Vindolanda tablets mention many different people. Sometimes they are referred to by their military rank and sometimes by their personal name. Roman names included a first name and several family names. The most popular boys' names were Lucius, Gaius and Marcus while most girls' names were a male name with a letter 'a' on the end, for example Claudia, the female version of Claudius.

Latin greetings
salve hello
salvete omnes hello everyone
ut vales? how are you?
bene vale keep well
vale goodbye

Soldiers were not meant to get married while they were in the army. This military certificate (from Cheshire) was issued in AD 103 to Reburrus, a Spanish officer in the 1st Pannonian cavalry regiment, when he left the army. As well as making him a Roman citizen the certificate says that he may now get married. However, the words say he may marry a future or present wife which suggests that he has an unofficial wife already!

15

shallow dishes 2,
side-plates 5,
vinegar-bowls 3,
 egg-cups 3,
on the shelf,
a platter,
a shallow dish,
a strong-box and
a bronze lamp,
bread-baskets 4,
cups 2,
in a box, bowls 2.

This is a list of everyday household objects. Many of them were used for cooking, eating or drinking. The tablet was found in a kitchen. The number of items seems very small for a fort full of soldiers, so perhaps this is a list for just one cupboard in the kitchen.

The list does not always say what the objects are made from, but archaeologists think that most of the objects at Vindolanda were probably pottery, with a few bronze utensils and lamps. It is unlikely that the fort used any silver objects for eating and drinking.

This late Roman silver pepper pot, fluted bowl and set of spoons were found buried in Suffolk. The wealthy owner of these objects would have used them on special occasions such as dining parties.

Making pots in Roman Britain was very organized and standard shapes were produced quickly and in large numbers. Most ordinary pots were multi-purpose containers which could be used for storing, preparing or cooking food. They were made across Britain wherever there was suitable clay.

Fine decorated pottery, such as Samian ware, was used as tableware. Most Samian ware was made in Gaul (modern France) and traded over wide areas including Britain.

Cooking ingredients were often mixed in gritted bowls (mortaria) to blend the flavours. Mortaria first appear in Britain before the Roman conquest, suggesting that a few people in Iron Age Britain were enjoying Roman recipes. This mortarium has the name of the potter who made it, Sollus, stamped on the rim.

This little bronze pan is decorated with colourful enamel and an inscription which reads: MAIS (Bowness-on-Solway) COGGABATA (Drumburgh) VXELODVNVM (Stanwix) CAMMOGLANNA (Castlesteads) RIGORE VALI AELI DRACONIS. These are the names of forts on Hadrian's Wall and the pan may be a souvenir belonging to a soldier called Draco who served on the Wall.

FOOD

*2 modii of bruised beans, 20 chickens, 100 apples, if you can find nice ones,
100 or 200 eggs, if they are for sale at a fair price,
8 sextarii of fish-sauce, a modius of olives.*

Vindolanda fort had large granaries which could store enough grain to feed the soldiers for many months. In addition, pigs and cattle in the local fields provided meat and milk (which could be made into butter or cheese). However, the fort was not able to provide all its own food and food was regularly bought from local traders. This tablet is a shopping list. The writer is quite particular, saying that they will only buy apples if they are nice ones!

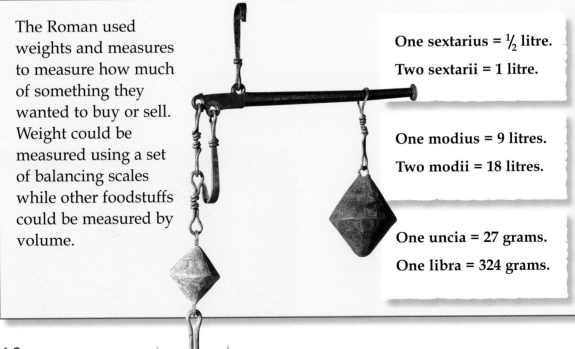

The Roman used weights and measures to measure how much of something they wanted to buy or sell. Weight could be measured using a set of balancing scales while other foodstuffs could be measured by volume.

One sextarius = ½ litre.
Two sextarii = 1 litre.

One modius = 9 litres.
Two modii = 18 litres.

One uncia = 27 grams.
One libra = 324 grams.

18

One tablet lists different foods, possibly as part of a recipe. The foods include garlic, spiced wine, salt and olives. These may be the ingredients for a tasty pickle.

Many different foods and drinks are listed on the tablets including: beans, lentils, bread, pancakes, barley, wheat, apples, eggs, porridge, chicken, pork-chops, fish, oysters, venison, ham, herbs, radishes, beetroot, butter, honey, spices, pepper, mustard, fish-sauce, olive oil, olives, vinegar, salt, garlic, wine and British beer.

One small tablet dated 15 August lists a pork cutlet, bread, wine and oil. Perhaps this was the dinner menu for the fort commander Flavius Cerialis on that day.

This tombstone was found near the Roman fort at Kirkby Thore, Cumbria. It was set up for the daughter of a soldier called Crescens. The tombstone shows a funeral banquet with the woman leaning back on a couch holding a two-handled cup while a servant passes her food from a small table.

19

KEEPING HEALTHY

Anise, nuts, berries, soft wheat-flour, beans, alum, wax, bitumen, bull's glue, pitch, blacking, anchusa, mustard-seed, verdigris, linen soaked in honey, resin, cumin, oak-gall.

This tablet is a list of items including food stuffs (such as flour and honey), raw materials (such as linen and bitumen) and natural products (such as berries and nuts). They were possibly used to make medicine for soldiers who were injured or unwell.

Another tablet mentions that some soldiers have eye infections. This small stone stamp (left) was used for marking sticks of eye-ointment. In a large fort like Vindolanda there was usually a hospital and one tablet mentions Marcus the doctor. This set of surgical instruments from Italy shows the type of medical tools used to treat soldiers injured in accidents and battle.

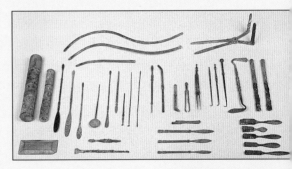

As well as the soldiers, the women and children living at the fort had to look after their health. In one tablet a woman called Paterna writes to Lepidina to say that she will bring her two remedies, one of them to help cure fever. It seems as if somebody in the commander's household was ill, perhaps one of the children.

The Romans also asked the gods to make them better. This altar was set up for the commander of the 20th Legion at Chester, perhaps because he was ill. It is dedicated to Aesculapius, the main Roman healing god (right), and Salus, the goddess of health.

The Romans believed that good hygiene was important for good health. A large Roman fort had baths and toilets with a sewage system to take the waste away. At Vindolanda a large bath house has been found where bathers might take their own oil and personal scrapers for cleaning themselves (right).

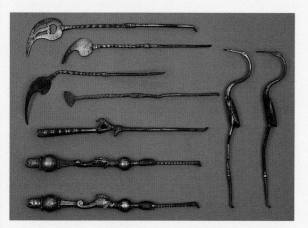

At home, people might have mirrors, combs and small metal kits with an ear scoop and nail cleaner (left).

Cavalry soldiers would take part in sporting events which were used as training sessions and to entertain the soldiers. These objects, found at Ribchester Roman fort, probably belonged to a cavalry soldier and include cavalry equipment and military awards. The helmet would have been decorated with streamers and worn at sports events.

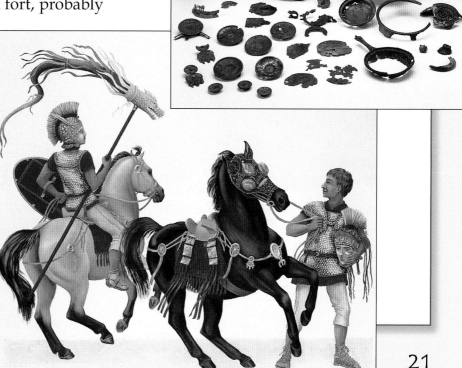

21

CLOTHING

I have sent you some socks from Sattua, two pairs of sandals and two pairs of underpants.

This letter was sent to a soldier serving at Vindolanda. The soldiers were given armour by the army but it appears they had to provide their own socks and pants. Auxiliary soldiers wore tunics and trousers under their armour. Thick overcoats were ordered for the soldiers to wear in cold weather and tombstones show them wearing thick neck scarves.

Many leather shoes have been found at Vindolanda. This child's shoe, found in London, shows the loops along each side used to lace it up over the foot.

Roman shoes and boots had metal studs on the bottom to stop the sole wearing out too quickly and broken shoes would be repaired at the fort.

The commander's wife and children brought their own clothing with them when they travelled to Britain. Roman women wore a long tunic with a shawl over the shoulders. This woman from Roman Egypt (left) is wearing jewellery made of gold. Gold jewellery was found with other treasures (right) near the east end of Hadrian's Wall.

Women's hairstyles often copied the hairstyles of the Imperial family. This coin shows Faustina, the wife of the emperor Marcus Aurelius, with her hair pulled back into a bun. Hairstyles were held in place with long hair pins. This one is a hairpin with its own hair-do!

Most clothes in Roman Britain were made from woollen or linen fabric. Pins and brooches were used to fasten both men and women's clothes and could be highly decorative. This brooch is in the shape of a dragon, a favourite design in Roman Britain. It would probably have been used to pin a thick woollen cloak.

You ought to decide, my lord, what quantity of wagons you are going to send to carry stone. Unless you ask Vocontius to sort out the stone, he will not sort it out. I ask you to write back to tell me what you want me to do.

The writer of this tablet is trying to organize the transport of some stone and he is waiting to hear how many wagons will be available. The wagons were pulled by horses. Nailed horseshoes were rarely used by the Romans. Instead iron hipposandals, a form of temporary shoe (right), were fastened to the horses' hooves.

Roman roads were used by officials with documents to deliver and government duties to perform, by soldiers moving between forts, and by traders carrying goods to sell. The first roads in a new province were built by the army, after which the local government had to look after the roads and build any new ones. Roman roads were made of several layers of stone and gravel and were built with a slightly curved surface and ditches on either side. This meant that rainwater ran off the stone surface, so that the road could be used in all weathers.

Soldiers were paid for their work in the army. The soldiers at Vindolanda were auxiliary soldiers and they were paid less than soldiers in the legions. Soldiers were usually paid with coins. This hoard of coins from Oxfordshire represents about 14 years of wages for an ordinary soldier.

The army was highly organized and even minor matters, such as soldiers asking for leave, had to be written down. Using the tablets from Vindolanda, experts have worked out that the army in Britain generated millions of documents. Only a few survive today, which is why the Vindolanda tablets are so important.

The Latin handwriting script on the tablets is known as 'Old Roman Cursive', a type of writing used for documents and letters between AD 1 and 300. The Romans used a range of materials for everyday documents. For quick notes pieces of pottery, known as ostraka, were used.

Wooden tablets covered with a layer of wax were a common type of portable document. A metal stylus was used to write on the soft wax which could be smoothed over and re-used.

The Romans used symbols for their numbers.

I for 1

V for 5

X for 10

C for 100

M for 1000

These symbols could be put together to make other numbers. This roof tile was made in the workshop of the 20th Legion. It is marked with a boar, the symbol of the legion, and LEG (Legion) XX (20).

Severus to his Candidus, greetings.
Regarding the dish for the Saturnalia, I ask you to buy it at a price of four or six asses and radishes to the value of not less than $\frac{1}{2}$ denarius.
Farewell.

Saturnalia was a Roman festival which took place on 17 December in honour of the god Saturn. The festival was celebrated by giving gifts and holding a banquet.

It was also a time when slaves were allowed more freedom than usual and the masters would wait on the slaves at the banquet. This letter is from Severus, a junior officer, to Candidus, a slave. Candidus would have been particularly looking forward to this festival! The radish was one vegetable which could still be gathered fresh at this time of year.

Roman holidays generally celebrated a certain god or goddess or mythical event. One Vindolanda tablet talks about the food for a summer festival in honour of a Roman goddess. Occasionally the soldiers held religious parades in honour of a god, especially Jupiter (left) or Mars. There were also parades on the emperor's birthday and when the soldiers were inspected by a high official or even the governor of Britain himself.

The Romans had special names for three of the days in a month. These were the Kalends (first day of the month), Nones (usually the 7th day of the month) and Ides (usually the 15th day of the month). These were believed to be important times in the calendar and in one tablet the writer comments that they have made sacrifices in honour of the day of the Kalends. This was probably New Year's Day which was a special day when people would wish each other a fortunate and happy New Year.

Throughout the year the Romans worshipped many different gods and goddesses. These small statues show some of them including the warrior god Mars on the far right. Even the emperor was worshipped as a god and this coin shows the emperor Trajan and his wife Plotina who were both deified (declared a god) when they died.

The god Mithras was popular with soldiers and along Hadrian's wall, three temples in honour of Mithras have been found at Housesteads, Carrawburgh and Rudchester forts.

This sculpture illustrates the myth about Mithras and the sacred bull.

As befits an honest man I implore your majesty not to allow me, an innocent man, to have been beaten with rods and, my lord, I was unable to complain to the prefect because he was detained by ill-health and I have complained in vain to the senior officer's assistant and the rest of the centurions of his unit. Accordingly I implore your mercifulness not to allow me, a man from overseas and an innocent one, about whose good name you may inquire, to be beaten by rods as if I had committed some crime.

This letter is from a trader who appears to have been badly treated by the army. He is probably writing to the governor of the province, for justice after a disagreement about the quality of the goods he is selling. In another letter, Octavius (a trader who buys supplies for the army) asks to be repaid the money he has spent on grain for the fort, so it appears that sometimes people were not paid money they were owed.

In another tablet somebody complains that their belt has been stolen. This bronze buckle was probably from the belt of an army officer at a Yorkshire fort during the late Roman period. It is decorated with a pair of sea-horses in the middle with dolphins on the outside. If the belt buckle was as fine as this one, the owner of the Vindolanda belt was probably more annoyed that the metal buckle had been stolen than the leather belt itself.

Not all complaints are about money and possessions. On one tablet Flavius Cerialis writes to his friend Caecilius September 'Tomorrow, which is 5 October, as you wish my lord, I will provide some goods by means of which we may endure the storms even if they are troublesome.' It would seem that the soldiers at Vindolanda were expecting some stormy autumn weather. Sometimes friends moan about each other. Sollemnis writes to his friend Paris complaining that he has not received a single letter back in reply to all the letters he has written to Paris.

Letters were also a way to ask for something nice to happen. In one fragment a woman called Valatta writes to the fort commander Cerialis asking him for a favour. Most of the writing is missing so we do not know what she was asking for, or if Cerialis said yes.

Even on an almost complete tablet, like this one, part of the writing may be missing if the tablet is damaged. Sometimes experts can work out what the missing letters or word might be. Other letters will always remain a mystery!

FURTHER READING

British Museum Pocket Timeline of Ancient Rome, Katharine Wiltshire, 2005

British Museum Illustrated Encyclopaedia of Ancient Rome, Mike Corbishley, 2003

British Museum Pocket Dictionary of Roman Emperors, Paul Roberts, 2006

British Museum Pocket Dictionary of Greek and Roman Gods and Goddesses, Richard Woff, 2003

FOR OLDER READERS

Life and Letters on the Roman Frontier: Vindolanda and its People by Alan Bowman, 2003

Garrison Life at Vindolanda: A Band of Brothers by Anthony Birley, 2002

WEBSITES

www.britishmuseum.org
British Museum website

www.britishmuseum.org/explore
Explore is an online database of over 5000 objects from the Museum's collections.

www.ancientcivilizations.co.uk
Ancient Civilizations website is an interactive learning and information website with text, images and maps relating to a range of civilizations across the world and through time. The site includes information on Roman Britain.

www.finds.org.uk
Portable Antiquities Scheme: look for Roman finds in your area on the PAS database and learn about being an archaeologist.

VISIT INFORMATION

The **British Museum** in London has many Roman objects, from Roman Britain and across the Roman empire, on display in its galleries. For more information about visiting the Museum, go to the Museum website. **www.britishmuseum.org**

Vindolanda Roman Fort is a few miles south of Hadrian's Wall. It is privately owned. Information about the site can be found on their website. **www.vindolanda.com**

Hadrian's Wall is a World Heritage Site. You can find out more about the 14 forts and museums, the Hadrian's Wall Path National Trail and the Hadrian's Wall Cycleway at **www.hadrians-wall.org**. Some sections of the Wall and some Wall forts are looked after by English Heritage. More information can be found on the English Heritage website at **www.english-heritage.org.uk**

TABLET INFORMATION

The Vindolanda tablets were recovered in fragments and there are often sections of writing missing where a tablet is broken or the writing has faded away. The tablets were deciphered by Prof. Alan Bowman and Prof. David Thomas. The English translations in this book are simplified versions with modern punctuation added. The complete texts, and notes about the translations, can be found on the Vindolanda tablet website at **www.vindolanda.csad.ox.ac.uk**

INDEX